Ghost hunting
South-West

Michael Williams

Bossiney Books · Launceston

Some other Bossiney books on related subjects

Dowsing in Devon and Cornwall by Alan Neal
Ghostly encounters South-West by Peter Underwood
Ghosts of Cornwall by Peter Underwood
Ghosts of Devon by Peter Underwood
Ghosts of Dorset by Peter Underwood
Ghosts of North Devon by Peter Underwood
Ghosts of Somerset by Peter Underwood
Psychic phenomena of the West by Michael Williams
Spiritual guides in the West Country by Jane E White
Supernatural Dartmoor by Michael Williams
Supernatural in the West by Michael Williams
UFOs over Devon by Jonathan Downes
Weird Devon by Jonathan Downes

Acknowledgements

I am deeply grateful to the people, especially members of the Ghost Club Society, who have given me interviews and authors who have allowed me to quote from their works. Thanks also to my wife Sonia and to Elaine Beckton who have been allies on so many projects – and last but not least to Jane and Paul White for the chance to write once more for Bossiney.

First published 2003 by
Bossiney Books Ltd, Langore, Launceston, Cornwall PL15 8LD
www.bossineybooks.co.uk
ISBN 1-899383-61-1
© 2003 Michael Williams
Printed in Great Britain by R Booth (Troutbeck Press), Mabe, Cornwall

Ghost hunting – a curious business

Ghost hunting *is* a curious business. There are various problems – so many that I sometimes wonder why sane men and women devote hours to the cause.

Firstly, there is an amazing diversity of phantoms and no total agreement on the definition of a ghost. Secondly, the attitude of owners of haunted properties varies enormously: some positively welcome a serious investigation; others slam the door in our faces – perhaps not literally but there is often a fear (sometimes unspoken) of unleashing further manifestation. The attitude of the press, radio and television can also vary, and in my experience the presence of the media during investigations tends to get in the way. This is extremely disappointing, because those of us who are serious in our quest hope that one day ghosts will be 'caught' on film; the more public the confirmation, the better.

Outside and beyond all this, ghosts seem shy characters, unable or unwilling to co-operate with investigators turning up at an appointed hour on a particular date.

I consider myself to occupy what I would call the 'middle ground'. On the one side you have the cynical Doubting Thomas, and on the other, the enthusiast who is inclined to be uncritical – and sometimes gullible. Those of us in the middle hopefully work with a sense of balance and objectivity, and I am grateful for the opportunity of having operated with Peter Underwood and Trevor Kenward, two immensely experienced ghost hunters both of whom examine hauntings with remarkable impartiality.

By all means let ghost hunters invest in cameras, tape recorders and any device that will help, but at the heart of any psychical research lie the character and calibre of the individual – and we salute pioneers like Edward Benson, the first bishop of Truro who later became Archbishop of Canterbury, the Reverend Sabine Baring-Gould, Sir Arthur Conan Doyle, Harry Price and others who have gone before us. Robert Stephen

Hawker, the vicar of Morwenstow, was another deeply interested in the paranormal.

The make-up of the team is supremely important. The ideal is a small unit operating in pairs, thereby ensuring there is more than one person present when a sighting occurs. The best ghost hunts are planned with the precision of a military operation, and procedures, timings, choice of pairs, etc are sometimes announced in advance. Enthusiasm is fine, but keeping one's feet on the ground and retaining objectivity are equally essential. People with a nervous disposition or a vivid imagination can be a handicap.

Anything unusual should be noted, reported and written down – often a happening on its own can appear relatively unimportant, but collectively such happenings may add up to something quite significant and intriguing. Naturally if anything can be recorded on a tape recorder or on film, so much the better.

The quest for evidence and proof

The dramatic rise in the number of television programmes on ghosts and allied subjects represents an important shift in public opinion – and the media's response to this growing interest in the paranormal. When I began investigating there were many people who ridiculed the subject and dismissed the investigators as 'crackpots'. Today, however, more and more men and women from all walks of life are beginning to accept the *facts* – paranormal events are not tales from long ago, but are taking place in the here and now.

The most infuriating aspect of ghost hunting, though, is the difficulty in obtaining proof which will satisfy the scientist. After nearly forty years of investigating and researching 'the other world' I have no doubt whatsoever about the reality of ghosts. But providing concrete evidence is another matter.

I have seen the print of a photograph taken by a Cornish vicar in his West Cornwall church. It was the priest's intention to photograph the font – and this he did, but when the photograph was eventually printed he had a shock. Standing beside the font was a lady in Elizabethan dress. She had not been visible to his naked eye when he had clicked his camera. As far as the vicar was concerned he was the only person in the building at the time.

From the scientific point of view, it's unlikely this series of events could be satisfactorily reproduced again – snaps of ghosts don't happen to order! – so the vicar's photo would no doubt be inadmissible proof.

Though ghost hunting is an intriguing business – and on occasion an exciting experience – one has to admit many ghost hunts fail to achieve anything substantial or satisfying. To shed some light on why this might be so, I talked to Claire Wolferson, a medium in North Somerset who had developed the gift of communicating with what is commonly known as the fourth dimension. I asked her three pertinent questions and these are the replies she received. Claire insisted she was merely the messenger and that she was only relaying information from 'out there'. She obtained this remarkable dictation in September 1996.

Q   Why is it that ghosts fail to keep appointments?

A   The answer is that conditions are not conducive to materialisation, especially where a number of people are investigating. Each individual will be manifesting at their own electrical impulse and therefore setting up conflicting currents (these are not apparent to incarnating mortals, although some people, particularly 'mediums', are sensitive to them). The discarnate one wishing to manifest on the human plane will find it impossible to control the electrical forces at their disposal, for they will be too varied. However, a sudden drop in temperature may indicate that a discarnate one is attempting to manipulate available forces in order to achieve the delicate operation of creating a visible image of their astral self on the much lower wave length of Earth.

Q   Why is there relatively so little film or photographic evidence of ghosts?

A   Discarnates manifesting on Earth's wavelength are operating at a higher frequency than that of man and his photographic apparatus. Therefore it is unlikely that the speed of the camera will be fast enough to catch an image.

Having said that, there may in some instances come a moment when your ghost is at its lowest speed possible and if a lucky photographer happens to be at the precise spot and the lighting is correct then he will obtain a satisfactory result. But it will be recognised that it is very unlikely these circumstances will occur concurrently very often – but often enough to be worth mentioning the possibility.

The time will come, with the advance of photographic science, when astonishing results will be obtained and mankind will be assured of the continuance of life after the death of the physical body. And a great burden will have been lifted.

Q   Will future evidence of the reality of ghosts one day convince the scientists?

A   Undoubtedly this will come about when mankind has devised more delicate forms of apparatus for recording sound and visual phenomena presented by those discarnate ones from the fourth dimension who long for recognition on Earth from their new state of existence. This follows their transition from the earthly plane to that heavenly sphere to which God has ordained people shall go according to their evolutionary progress.

Many of these wish above all else to reassure sorrowing relatives and friends of their continued existence since the death of their physical selves. They long to explain that they manifest in bodies which are exact replicas of their earthly ones, except that they have no defects. This heavenly body is commonly named 'the astral body', and it is this which is seen by clairvoyants (a clairvoyant is one who has trained him or herself in former incarnations through much prayer and meditation to 'tune in' to the higher wavelength of the next dimension; in other words their brain acts as a radio set and receives the signal being 'broadcast' to it by discarnate ones).

Some of these discarnate entities may come not merely to identify themselves and describe their favourable circumstances, but to attempt to rectify some wrong they feel they have perpetrated, or to have some wish fulfilled, or to correct the interpretation of some historical event. These latter cases will meet with many difficulties and endure much frustration, for they are unlikely to make much headway in the materialistic world of man. Besides which, circumstances will almost certainly have changed, so there will be no tacit understanding between the communicators.

When communication exists more widely between this world and the next, which will come about in the next [21st] century, there will be a great change in the attitude of scientists, for proof of life after death will be indisputable. Moreover they will find themselves conversing with discarnate members of their own profession. This will be extremely rewarding, for their old friends will, with their new-found knowledge, provide answers to many a knotty problem which had defeated them on Earth.

All in all, a turning point will have been reached in the affairs of man, for not only will there no longer be a dread of death of the physical, with its agonising partings from loved ones, but there will be a new enlightenment throughout the world wherever credence is given to those enabled to make contact with the next dimension. Furthermore, it should be understood that Earth's electrical impulses, together with the rest of this solar system, are being heightened at God's ordination, although of necessity the undertaking has to be extremely slow (as viewed from Earth) to avoid undesirable repercussions within the universe.

To be or not to be - frightened

Why are some people frightened by ghosts, when others accept their appearance or disappearance with absolute calm?

It is an important question, and there is probably no short clearcut answer. Of course, I'm not referring to poltergeist activity – the word 'poltergeist' is derived from German, meaning 'noisy spirit'. Truth is, a poltergeist can be an extremely unpleasant character.

James Turner, an author friend, told me how he used to live in an old rectory that was, in his words, 'infected by poltergeists'. One day a key was flung into the hall from an upstairs bedroom and, though James returned the key to its rightful place on dozens of occasions, it was invariably thrown downstairs again. Coals, too, flew across landings and down the stairs.

In my experience most ghosts are quite friendly, but they seem reluctant to have a chat. In nearly forty years of investigating I have met only one man who engaged in conversation with a ghost – and they spoke mainly about the weather!

As time goes on, I take the view that many people who are frightened by ghosts are men and women who previously did not believe in them, in the same way that numerous characters who do not believe in the hereafter find themselves approaching death with apprehension and agitation.

When I saw phantom lights inside Bossiney Chapel, outside Tintagel, and the ghostly cyclist travelling along the Bodmin-Camelford road, or heard invisible footsteps in the cottage at Bossiney, I never felt a tremor of fear – and I say that in no boastful sense, because I'm sure some sightings can be very frightening. Eleanor Englefield, who lived at Rock near Wadebridge for a number of years, told me of such an experience.

'Back in 1945, I was stationed in Ilfracombe, in North Devon. I had a passion for walking and I decided to climb the Hangman Hills… There are two of them, 'The Lesser' and 'The Greater Hangman'. From the village of Coombe Martin it's about half an hour, fairly fast climbing. The village soon drops from sight under the shoulder of the hill and the climber is alone with wind and sun and glorious scenery. Leaving the lesser hill on my left, I began to approach the main summit and, with surprise, noticed that the grass ended quite abruptly… a circle of stony ground crowned the top of the hill.

'I remember thinking in a disinterested way that the altitude was surely not as high as that. At any rate I crossed the boundary between grass and stony ground, and started the last ascent. Everything was all right until I saw the small cairn of stones. I wish I could describe the shape exactly, but I cannot. It was, very roughly, the same structure as a Cornish cross. My first thought was that some child had been playing with the stones, but I knew that was ridiculous; no child would play in this lonely place.

'Then I saw the second cairn, slightly larger than the first and just behind it. It was at that point the nightmare began to manifest itself. There were hundreds of things, varying from several centimetres in height to some over two metres high. They were all about me... and the terror they inspired was something I shall never forget. I knew I was utterly at the mercy of something that not only could, but would, annihilate me in a flick of time... something that resented me being there.

'I cannot pretend to understand what it was I faced on that brilliant day in June 1945. All I know is it had tremendous power, and I also knew that the thing I feared could only be seen by me in the shape of those stone cairns. They were the symbols that reflected the reality just as St John could see only the truth of God in weird beasts.

'Another odd thing is that the top of the hill had gone; I was facing a huge stony plain, stretching as far as the eye could see. I had stepped into another dimension with a vengeance. Suddenly, I thought of the Lord's Prayer – it was the only thing I could think of – and slowly and aloud I began to recite it. The rigidity left my limbs and I could move. I turned back. I was quite near the grass. The cairns were still about me, but they seemed to have receded.

'I started to walk. I knew – God knows how – that once I crossed on to the green grass I would be safe. As I walked, I was aware of something behind me, but I dared not look around. As I stepped on to the green turf, I knew that which followed had halted... it could not cross the boundary.

'As I hurried down the hill, I looked back. The stony hill crest was there... but nothing else...'

The diversity of ghosts

Ghosts defy neat, easy classification. Times were when it was generally accepted that a ghost was the spectre of someone who had died. But such a definition is inadequate. What about a ghost which haunts several quite different places? What about the ghost train in Somerset? And what about shapeless phantoms or recurring phenomena?

Some ghosts are so real that we don't recognise them as ghosts. James Turner, who lived his last years in a house in St Teath village, told me of one such experience in his London days. He was working as a secretary to a lady who managed advertising catalogues for some upmarket London firms and who also owned a magazine, which James edited. During the day James worked in her flat near Olympia – one room had been converted into an office. Each afternoon he left at 5 pm and he would leave on his desk any correspondence or related matters he had not finished so that Miss Smith (as he called her), who came in for two hours in the evening, might complete the work.

Now James had never met Miss Smith, but he knew she had been because each morning the letters and scripts would all be neatly typed. 'One evening I was a little late in leaving. When I opened the front door of the flat to go to the lift, this young girl was standing outside about to ring the bell. She was dressed very correctly and carrying a brief case. I nodded to her, said "Good evening" and held the door for her to go inside. I remember she had a very pleasant smile.'

So, thought James, I have at last seen the famous Miss Smith. But next morning he had a surprise. The letters left on his desk were untouched. In a telephone call to his employer James explained he had let her in on the previous evening.

'Impossible,' said his boss, 'Miss Smith rang me to say she was in bed with flu.'

Nothing was stolen, and James's description matched the real Miss Smith. He came to one conclusion: he had seen that rare character – the ghost of a living person.

It has been estimated that about one person in ten stands a chance of seeing a ghost. That may seem a high percentage but, as the James Turner experience shows, many people initially are unaware of a ghostly presence – they believe they are seeing an ordinary human being, not a phantom.

The case of Captain D M Swetnam, a Master Mariner, is typical. He lived in a ground floor flat in Penzance with his wife. He told me, 'My wife was taken ill and, being restless one night and not wishing to disturb her, I got up, made myself a cuppa and sat down in the lounge to read for a while. Suddenly I sensed I was not alone. Glancing up it was to see a strikingly beautiful young woman in a white embroidered ball gown, walking across from a door which led out into the garden – such as it was – and continuing, seemingly, right through the door jamb of the adjoining kitchen and on into the spare bedroom next door.'

Soon after, Captain Swetnam went back to sea for about three months, and 'returning home to find my wife living with only part of the electrics functional, took myself down to the cellars to trace the fault. Entrance to these was from an inner sort of courtyard down some very wet and steep stone steps. Having navigated these, I was probing around, lit only by a torch, when I glanced up and another apparition seemed to have joined me.

'This time, sad to say, it was not the lovely young lass of before, but what I can only describe as a piratical-looking customer who walked across in front of me and, seemingly, on through a solid stone wall.'

Later Captain Swetnam discussed the sightings with a man who ran a Penzance antiques shop. This man, having good local knowledge, shed some light on the second incident, but knew nothing about the young lady in the ball gown.

'He told me I was not the first to see the pirate and the popular thought was that it was a cellarman who fell or was pushed down the steps and "brained" himself on the stone doorpost. It had, apparently, been the subject of a police enquiry and something of a scandal, but nothing was ever proved.

'After this second effort, I did get round to telling my wife about both incidents, fully expecting her to react with all the usual jokes about taking more water with it, etc. But instead, she took me quite seriously and told me that, whilst she had seen nothing, a couple of times when I had been away at sea she had suddenly felt someone else was in the room and it had gone bitterly cold even though it was the middle of summer.'

Other ghosts are sometimes little more than a suggestion. The Eliot Arms – also known as The Square and Compass – at Tregadillet near Launceston has such a manifestation.

It all began in 1995 when it was decided to level the floor in the lounge-dining area. When Phil the builder was working there, on occasions he was aware of an unseen presence as if an invisible someone was watching him. Then one morning something or someone came into the room through the door by the clock. 'A white shadow' was how he described it.

Soon after, the then joint landlord Les Eliot saw a similar fleeting spirit. He, too, thought of it in terms of 'a white shadow'. Then Stephanie Barrett, who works there, saw the same 'white or grey shadow but there was a very distinct shoulder… oddly like a fraction of someone's body'.

One manifestation coincided with the alarm system going off. 'An impossible situation,' Les explained, 'because the system was off at the time.' Angela, who works in the kitchen, also swears she saw this barely visible phantom come into the dining room area via a solid wall.

Outside and beyond all this, a brace of goblets disappeared from their display position by one of the windows in the same room and, more incredibly, reappeared a fortnight later. Various objects have been moved from their original places but, rather strangely, without damage – almost as if they had been gently and carefully moved on purpose rather than falling accidentally.

The inn, which was a masons' lodge for French prisoners during the Napoleonic wars (the French prisoners worked on local farms and some of them stayed in Cornwall), stands on two ley lines – this information comes from a highly respected dowser over the border in Devon. The oldest part of the building dates from the 14th century; there was further development in the 16th century, and a third phase two hundred years later. So a strong sense of the past hangs about the place – you get the impression something of a paranormal nature could happen at any time but in a quiet fashion.

In the autumn of 2002 I paid a return visit to the Eliot Arms and discovered there has been an increased amount of supernatural activity in the last two years.

Landlady Debbie Cooper and her partner Jamie Player told me that there have been sightings of a small girl and an elderly lady dressed in Victorian costume – and singing by invisible females has been heard.

All of this has been confirmed by a fellow Ghost Club Society member Richard Tucker who works at the inn. The Eliot Arms is clearly one of those properties with an ongoing reputation.

There is a school of thought that ghosts are more likely to manifest on or near water. Certainly here in the West Country there is a lot of evidence to support that theory.

Joan Bettinson, who lives at Commonmoor on Bodmin Moor, had this strange experience. 'It was a grey day, the second week in July 1989, with a brisk wind blowing from the west. Dick and Ruby, our friends, picked us up, Jack my husband and me, between two and three o'clock for an afternoon and evening's fishing at Siblyback Lake, as we often did. Siblyback was deserted but for two fishermen on the west bank.

'We wandered down the bank on the east side. Dick and Jack were able to fish but it was too strong a wind for Ruby and me, so we made our way over the dam where we had a full view of the whole area. There was no one at all on the bridge, but on getting halfway across… as if from nowhere we saw a figure coming *slowly* towards us, head bent. I looked down momentarily at a blob of what birds do and looked up. The figure had gone! No sign of anyone. He – we thought it was a man – definitely did not pass us and he could not have turned and retraced his steps without being seen.

'Ruby was quite scared. We carried on over, both feeling nervous. When our men eventually joined us, we asked if anybody had passed them. "No" was, of course, their answer. I walked up to the other two anglers who were still fishing, but neither had seen anyone. We thought it was the ghost of a fisherman. It could have been a chap who spent many hours fishing here, and when he died his ashes were thrown on the lake.

'A couple of days later I was talking to two friends Nigel and Walt, and Nigel said, "Funny thing… we were there yesterday with our four dogs, and we began to cross the bridge. At about the same spot all four dogs lay down and would not move. In the end they turned round and went bounding off… they had never done that before."

'Looking back, I have always found Siblyback an eerie place… it was inhabited 5000 years ago by ancient man. There used to be a quarry not far from the bridge and a local farmer told us a man was killed there. So who was it – the dead quarryman or the fisherman who loved the place? I think it was the fisherman!'

Travelling ghosts

My interest in travelling ghosts dates back to the early 1970s when I interviewed a man called Patrick Humpherson who had had a strange experience on the old road which sliced Bodmin Moor.

He was driving a car between Five Lanes and Jamaica Inn, and recalled: 'I hadn't been aware of anything on the road ahead when, without warning, an old green car came from nowhere and overtook me on the nearside. I had no time to brake or swerve, nor could I have done anything. It was alongside me and then gone in a flash! But in those few brief seconds I saw it as a very old open car with hood pulled back, and its four occupants were young men who were singing boisterously and half standing on their seats. The passenger in the back, furthest from me, had a hat in his hand.

'The car didn't have any headlights, and the only indication of lighting was an old brass lamp, the old oil type fitted between the door and windscreen. I expect I swore at these seemingly crazy idiots for passing me on the wrong side and I eased my speed, somehow half expecting something else to come along, but nothing did and I went on to Falmouth without further incident.

'The years went on, but I never got the sight of that car out of my mind. Certain details stood out very clearly. I cannot remember any engine noise but I have the distinct memory of happy singing, and one of the men, in his half-standing position, the one nearest to me, was wearing a three-quarter length brown tweed coat.

'Then one day I came into the company of a group of coach drivers – we were in the car park at St Ives – and there was the usual amount of leg pulling, which was mainly directed at one man, a serious type who kept repeating an experience he'd had the previous night. I enquired and was told he'd encountered a ghost car when he was travelling from Tavistock to Liskeard. I at once naturally became very interested and asked a few questions, and soon learned that this driver had had the same experience as me many years before – though his experience had been some miles from mine. Before meeting this man, I had never told anyone of my encounter with the phantom car. But he gave me the same description, and the car and the occupants were the same as those I had seen.'

Interest in the subject deepened on a November afternoon in 1984. It was early afternoon – very clear visibility and on one of those almost empty November roads in Cornwall. I had been doing business down on the south coast and was driving along the Bodmin to Camelford road when I saw this cyclist coming in the opposite direction, from Camelford.

There was nothing vague or misty about the man or his cycle, but suddenly they were no longer on the road – there one moment and gone the next. I was certain we had not passed one another. Immediately my paranormal instincts were roused and I turned the van around and drove more than half a mile back along the road, but there was no sign of the cyclist – I am sure that in the time scale he could not have reached the next side turning. Moreover on reflection he, his clothes and his cycle all seemed of an earlier time, and they were all grey – as if one were looking at a photograph in an old family album.

Soon after that November afternoon sighting I was speaking to a group of people in North Cornwall, on the subject of paranormal activity in the West Country. One of the audience told me how only a few days before he had been driving along the road near Bude and had been aware of another car following him. A few moments later, when he looked in the driver's mirror, there was no sign of the following car. He was quite convinced it had simply vanished, and expressed the view that a tiny percentage of the cars we see travelling on our roads may be ghost vehicles.

In October 2001 I had a brief but vivid experience in the lanes near Helston. Driving back to St Teath, I saw this grey van coming up the lane in the opposite direction. I halted my car at a suitable spot to let the van pass when suddenly the van vanished. The manifestation lasted probably less than half a minute, but I have no doubt about the reality of it. It was 4.30 in the afternoon and visibility was excellent.

It is an interesting and established paranormal fact that some ghosts manifest themselves for a period of time and then apparently fade from the scene. The phantom hitchhiker in Somerset is such a case. He was seen by various motorists in the 1950s and again in the 1970s, but I have heard of no sightings of this strange character more recently – he was strange in that he appeared by the roadside, usually in very heavy rain between Wellington and Taunton. One driver picked him up and put him down at the requested stopping place only to encounter him some miles further up the Taunton road – yet no vehicle had overtaken the lorry. There is no doubt some ghosts do manifest themselves in certain weather conditions, for example, ghostly sounds of horses and a carriage at St Just-in-Penwith, West Cornwall – and these are heard only in stormy weather.

Do some ghosts leave a message? Many people in London

believed a number 7 bus seen in the Ladbroke Road area in the 1930s had such a message. Dozens of people saw this huge run-away red bus careering down an empty road at night long after other buses had stopped running. It looked very real but did not have a driver or passengers, caused several accidents and a death, and was seen by some as a 'sign'. Observers believed this travelling ghost was telling the borough council to straighten a dangerous bend where accidents had occurred. They maintained there was a blind corner at the junction of St Mark's Road and Cambridge Gardens where the real number 7 bus ran during its working day. In due course the council knocked down the wall and widened the junction – and the ghost bus was never seen again.

Ghosts of famous characters in the West

Some time ago a media man, cynical on the subject of paranormal possibility, challenged me: 'Why are these ghosts always famous personalities and not ordinary people? Nobody says "that's the ghost of old Joe Bloggs down at Redruth…"'

I was rather amused by it all because the great majority of ghosts are those of ordinary people – so ordinary that we do not know their identity. Only a few days before this media encounter a psychic told me how he had recently been engaged in detailed conversation with a long dead Cornish farmer who was worried about a missing bullock. You can hardly be more down to earth than that. My files bulge with 'ordinary' ghosts: the unknown murdered customer at Jamaica Inn, the old seaman at the Bush Inn, the butler at Tredethy Country Hotel, and the tall figure seen by Ludgvan churchyard are just four of many Cornish ghosts which come into this category.

Nevertheless *some* of our West Country ghosts are those of well-known characters and I propose to devote this chapter to five of them, one of whom has achieved celebrity status by becoming a phantom. What would our media man make of that?

Arguably the most famous West Country ghost is that of

Lawrence of Arabia in Dorset. After a first-class degree in history at Oxford University, Lawrence's love affair with Arabia began through archaeology. His knowledge of Egypt meant that within months of the outbreak of war in 1914 he found himself in Cairo as an army officer. With the Turks siding with the Germans, Britain needed a man who could recruit support among the middle eastern Arabs. T E Lawrence was their man. Leading guerrilla attacks, and motivating the Arab communities, he soon became a legendary figure. Captured and brutalised by the Turks, Lawrence escaped and took part in a victory parade in Jerusalem. He left the army a hero, and a colonel, but declined to accept the Order of the Bath and the DSO from King George V.

This refusal reflected his complex character.

After flirting with fame (in 1922 his memoirs, *The Seven Pillars of Wisdom*, were published), he made desperate attempts to withdraw from public life. First he joined the RAF under an assumed name as an ordinary aircraftsman. When his true identity was discovered, he left the RAF and enlisted in the tank corps, again under a false name. He then went back to the RAF and was eventually discharged in 1935. At the age of 45 he was facing retirement.

By then he had established his own little Mecca in the Dorset countryside: 'the cottage is alone in a dip in the moor, very quiet, very lonely, very bare...' he later wrote, 'Wild horses would not take me away from Clouds Hill. It is an earthly paradise.'

But it was not to last. On 13 May 1935 he left Clouds Hill on his motor cycle, rounded a hill and crashed. The accident proved fatal. There was much controversy surrounding Lawrence's death – some people suspected foul play, as it transpired his friend Henry Williamson had supposedly sent a letter to him (it was never found) in which he suggested Lawrence should meet with Hitler. Williamson supported the British Fascist Movement and believed an exceptional man like Lawrence would have a beneficial impact on Hitler. Lawrence was to meet Williamson the next day, but of course 'fate' prevented any meeting from taking place.

The puzzling circumstances surrounding Lawrence's death have still not been unravelled to the satisfaction of those keen to reveal the real truth behind this most enigmatic of men.

Over the years people have been certain that they have seen Lawrence's ghost – an Arab-like, white-robed figure – entering his cottage. Others insist they have heard the ghostly roar of a motorcycle – on the road where he had his accident.

Dorset's other celebrity ghost is that of George Jeffreys – Judge Jeffreys, who achieved notoriety for his ruthless sentencing, especially his treatment of rebels who took part in Monmouth's rebellion. They called him 'Bloody Judge Jeffreys', and with good reason. He was hated all over the West Country, and continues to send psychic shivers through the county. His ghost has been seen in Lyme Regis, wearing robes, wig and black cap. In Dorchester he has been seen at night in a supermarket, in the region of the meat counter! And some people vow they have seen his face peering out of a window in a nearby passageway. Further afield, in Taunton, he is reputed to haunt the County Museum which is housed inside the old castle – the scene of Jeffreys's 'bloody assizes'.

The biggest disappointment of decades of researching into ghosts is I have never met or corresponded with anyone who has seen the ghost of Sir Francis Drake. Historically there have been reports of Sir Francis's ghost being seen at The Ship Inn, Martin's Lane, Exeter. It is feasible, because the inn was a favourite haunt of the famous sea dog; indeed it is said he drank there with famous Devon seamen like Sir Walter Raleigh, Sir John Hawkins and Sir Humphrey Gilbert.

We certainly know Sir Francis stayed at the inn in 1587, since in a letter despatched that year he wrote:

'Next to mine own shippe I do most love that old "Shippe" in Exon, a tavern in Fysshe Street, as the people call, or as the clergie will have it St Martin's Lane.

'There yestere'en I had some speech with a mariner fresh

come hither from Plimouth... the power of Spain is already afloat, so in the morning, please God, I am for Plimouth and for another Shippe than this.'

In November 1996 I talked with the landlord of The Ship who told me there had been no sightings in recent years, but he had distinctly heard footsteps walking across the restaurant upstairs when in fact that area was closed and nobody, either staff or customers, was present. But he had no doubt about the reality of the footsteps. The last positive sighting was by a cleaning lady in the 1980s who claimed to have been thrown down the stairs by a ghost! But a psychic friend says Sir Francis would not have done such a thing...

Having said that, within a supernatural context Sir Francis has had rather a bad press. He was – to many people – a magical figure; so much so that some Devonians believed he was in league with the Devil. They said he and his brother and sister wizards assembled at Devil's Point, that most westerly promontory at Plymouth, and conjured up the wicked storm which caused such havoc among the invading Spanish Armada.

Drake's famous drum is kept at his old home, Buckland Abbey near Yelverton, now a National Trust property. Apart from being one of Britain's most famous heirlooms, the drum is the subject of various tales which keep the spirit of Drake alive.

Robert Hunt, writing in the 19th century, observed that old Betty Donithorne, formerly the housekeeper of Buckland Abbey, assured him if Drake heard the drum beating *he rises and has a revel.*

Sir Henry Newbolt, knowing about the ancient superstitions surrounding Drake, turned them into patriotic words:

> Take my drum to England, hang it by the shore;
> Strike it when your powder's running low.
> If the Dons sight Devon, I'll quit the port of Heaven,
> And drum them up the Channel as we drummed them
>   long ago.

Such theories resurfaced during the Second World War. Back in 1940, when the Battle of Britain was raging, the BBC put out a programme – 'Drake's Drum'. It was broadcast on the overseas transmission. That September, as the Luftwaffe lost its fight for control of the daytime skies over Britain, two army officers swore they heard the drum again, beating defiantly on the coast-line of Hampshire. Plymouth residents, who escaped to the open countryside during the devastating air raids on the city, reported hearing drum beats from the north between bursts of anti-air-craft fire to the south. Some claimed it was a supernatural sound, but many firmly believed it was a gallant attempt by the authorities to summon Drake's support.

Can we dismiss this as all legend?

More and more people are inclining to the the view that King Arthur was a historical probability rather than a legendary fig-ure. Some historians go as far as to assert he was a genuine mil-itary leader here in the South-West. Not surprising then, that there have been reports of the ghostly figure of the King seen among the ruins of Tintagel Castle. Some say now and then the castle itself turns fleetingly from its present ruined condition into its former castle shape and glory and then back again to ruins.

A Dutch painter visiting Tintagel with his wife had a very strange experience on the cliffs. He gave detailed descriptions of a horse and rider he had seen galloping along the cliff path: the rider was stylishly dressed in a black, broad-brimmed hat, and boots with spurs. Husband and wife agreed on the details and the sequence of events: the horse and rider suddenly appearing as if from nowhere, then coming to a halt, the rider dismounting and tethering the reins to a low-lying branch – and then both vanishing into thin air.

'Was it Arthur?' asked the wife.

'Who else could it have been?' was the painter's reply.

I have no doubt about the authenticity of their sighting – too detailed to have been imagination or hallucination. But I doubt whether it were Arthur. From their description he was more likely a member of the Cornish gentry engaged in local smug-gling activity at a later date.

There have been reported sightings of a radiant female phantom in the vicinity of Glastonbury Tor in Somerset. There is a Glastonbury theory that she is Guinevere and it may be correct because there are accounts of an excavation at the abbey in the 1100s. A female skeleton was discovered, with long strands of golden hair still clinging to her skull. It is said the golden hair turned to dust when exposed to the air, and those golden tresses are reputed to be the source of the strange light in which her ghostly form is bathed.

At Cadbury there have been further reported sightings of Arthur's ghost accompanied by phantom knights and horses riding over the top of the hill and down to the spot where the gatehouse once stood. The key question is 'Can we dismiss all these reports as illusions?' I somehow doubt it and my hope is one day – or night – a convincing time slip relating to Camelot will occur in Somerset or Cornwall.

Finally, on to how a quite ordinary person became a celebrity by turning into a ghost.

Charlotte Dymond was only eighteen years old, working for Mrs Phillippa Peter, a widow in the parish of Davidstow, helping in the house and milking on the farm: a simple country girl of her time. There must have been dozens and dozens of such Cornish girls living and working on the farms on and around Bodmin Moor, but Charlotte had the ability to turn any man's head.

On a Sunday afternoon in April 1844 she walked with her limping lover Matthew Weeks on the moor. We shall never know why Charlotte tormented him that Sunday afternoon with talk of Tommy Prout whom she said flirted with her, and she mentioned one or two other boys from Davidstow – possibly inventions. What Charlotte did not know was that Matthew had a knife in his pocket. She went too far, and too late saw the madness in his eyes. There on the edge of the moor he cut her throat with one swift stroke of his knife.

That was the picture the prosecution painted at Matthew's trial – he had been arrested on Plymouth Hoe. He was found

'Guilty' and duly hanged.

But in 2002, on the anniversary of Charlotte's death, I, together with the well-known west country medium Pamela Smith-Rawnsley, and a fellow member of the Ghost Club Society, went to the murder spot.

Pamela, operating her pendulum, contacted Charlotte and uncovered the following.

'Did Matthew Weeks murder you?'

An emphatic 'No' and the admission that Matthew was forced into making some sort of confession.

'Did you know the identity of the murderer?'

Reply: 'Yes, he was a local man who wanted to establish a relationship with me but I felt unable to return his affection.'

'Was Matthew with you when the other man appeared?'

Reply: 'No, Matthew had gone back to the farm.'

We all formed the impression that Charlotte was on her way to an appointment, probably seeking work and accommodation on another part of the moor.

'Were you waylaid?'

Reply: 'Yes, this man waited until I was alone, and then made advances. He forced me down to a spot by the river and I turned away and in trying to get away from him I was attacked from behind.'

Today Charlotte is remembered by a simple monument below Rough Tor by the stream, and her fame increased as men and women swore they saw her ghost walking this part of the moor in early evening. Sentries of the Old Volunteers, encamped nearby, claimed they saw her ghost – so clearly that they were able to give detailed descriptions of the lone figure, which matched the clothing Charlotte Dymond was wearing on the last fateful Sunday afternoon.

I had one very odd experience on Rough Tor which may or may not have had something to do with the ghost of Charlotte Dymond. It was agreed I should do a feature for a magazine on Rough Tor and Brown Willy. Early one September morning, I set off, accompanied by photographer Bryan Russell and a tan and white terrier called Tex. Tex's presence, in a curious way, did two things: it ruined our expedition and, at the same time, helped to deepen my probings into supernatural subjects.

The higher we climbed, that beautiful September morning, the more apprehensive the little dog became – that in itself was strange because he was normally a pugnacious character. Once on top of Rough Tor, Bryan Russell got to work with his cameras, but Tex hid in a crevice.

Brown Willy, on the other side, had a wonderfully beckoning quality and, as the haze dissolved, sunlight rimmed the skyline. But Tex refused to go another inch. He shook like a seriously ill animal, and I became so concerned about his condition that we called off the whole project, deciding to carry Tex back to the car parked down by Rough Tor Farm and drive straight to Mr Byrne, the veterinary surgeon at Camelford. For once, Tex was happy to be carried: a four-legged parcel of agitation. His tremors were so violent I wondered if he was about to die.

Half-way down the slope, however, Tex started struggling. I gently placed him on the ground, and he scampered away, a totally different dog.

Did he detect something beyond our human vision that morning? Did he in fact see Charlotte's ghost?

Haunted Devon

Joan Amos is a keen and knowledgeable student of UFOs and psychic phenomena. She lived for many years in a small village, Peter Tavy, outside Tavistock before real Dartmoor begins. Joan has scrap books, cuttings and correspondence from all over the world. Few people, though, know that her Lucy Cottage has a history of strange goings-on.

She told me, 'A murdered boy lived here. He was killed walking home one evening many years ago and they brought him back and laid him out in the front room. When we first moved into this cottage, someone in Tavistock said to me: "I suppose you know that cottage is haunted!" I told my husband when I got home, but he just laughed and put it down to country superstition. We did not know at the time what had happened…

'Now whenever I show people this front room, it makes many of them shudder, even though they don't know why. No one likes to go into it and we have never really used it. When two girls from London came to stay overnight, they described it as a "cold spot".

'There are things that happen here that are unexplainable. One evening we were watching television when a photograph flipped up in the air, as if someone had deliberately flicked it up. Freddie, my husband, and I looked at each other in utter astonishment; we had to admit it was very strange. Now my dear Fred has gone, and I had my 19 year old grandson staying with me for a while. We both jumped out of our skin when a door slammed upstairs; yet I knew there were no doors or windows open, nor was there any wind blowing.

'When my grandson went into the kitchen one evening to make a cup of tea, a plastic jug flew off the hook at him; he looked so startled, saying "Who did that?" I laughed and said, "That's Freddie! He doesn't like anyone in his kitchen." I saw a nail brush jump off the soap dish at me, too.

'When I have anyone to stay, I don't tell them but I wait to hear what they have to say. Recently my sister-in-law said she could hear people downstairs talking; she thought I had left the radio on. There have been other times when the television set has misbehaved, turning itself on in the middle of the night. And then there was the mirror upstairs – it came crashing off the nail and shattered.

'Often I think I can hear someone walking about upstairs, when I know I am in the house alone. My cats often look at something, when there is nothing there. Mother cat bolts around the house scared stiff at times. And one day a visitor to the cottage saw a phantom long-haired grey cat. Personally, I've not seen the cat, but I have been aware of its presence on several occasions.'

Perhaps the biggest mystery of all relating to Lucy Cottage is the strange figure who passes the window – seen so clearly that

Joan and others have got up and gone to the kitchen door. 'But always the same result,' says Joan, 'nobody there.'

In a number of his books Tom Lethbridge explored the theory that there is a variety of field forces connecting woods and water, hills and open areas. He further suggested, if this were so, it would account for previously seemingly baffling appearances, emotions and experiences.

He firmly believed Nature is packed with odd tape recordings, dating back thousands of years, and that people can enter into or leave 'fields' of depression that were imprinted, often in water or humid places. Just as underground water exerts a magnetic field that can be picked up with a dowsing rod, so he suggested water can record and transmit strong emotions. And ghosts can also be associated with emotions. At a jumble sale in Branscombe village hall, Mina Lethbridge, an animal lover, noted a lady with her dog. Later she saw the lady leave, minus her dog, and she naturally went to see if an animal had been left behind – but there was no sign of any forgotten dog. It so happened that the lady's sister-in-law worked for the Lethbridges at Hole House. She confirmed that her sister-in-law now owned no dog, but the animal seen by Mina matched a much-loved pet who had died five years ago.

Finally, the case of a disappearing ghost – also in South Devon. Eileen McKenna, who at one time worked for the Lord Mayor of Birmingham, presided over the very successful Southern Cross Guest House at Newton Poppleford for a number of years. People travelled from all over Britain and from overseas to enjoy her delicious Devonshire cream teas, but not many knew of the two ghosts which resided at the guest house.

On many occasions Eileen was aware of a ghostly girl, aged about 18, and her shaggy dog. Their appearances were often sig-nalled by a creaking of the stairs or the lights going dim. And the proprietress was not alone in observing these sudden appear-ances and disappearances; a number of guests claimed they saw 'Nancy' and her pet.

After about nine years Eileen decided to extend Southern

Cross and behind one of the walls builders found an old staircase leading up to the roof. The staircase was removed and during the work 'Nancy' could be heard wailing and crying. Soon after, she disappeared for good. Some time after that a lady from Ottery St Mary contacted Eileen and explained that Nancy was her niece who had died in 1943.

Ghostly sounds and shared sightings

My study of ghostly sounds developed when we lived in a cottage alongside Bossiney Hotel, just outside Tintagel.

Probably more than thirty times my wife Sonia and I heard footsteps ascending the narrow staircase of the cottage – we never heard them descending – and often they were immediately preceded by the sound of a downstairs door opening. In reality we never found that door open at such times and as for the footsteps on the cottage stairs, they were so life-like that for some time we assumed one of us was coming up the stairs. Not once did we see anyone, but a neighbour, Mary Bower, who lived in a bungalow in Bossiney Lane, was convinced the footsteps belonged to the ghost of a young girl who years earlier had crashed down the staircase – to her death.

It is an intriguing paranormal fact that when ghosts walk they often stick to old routes. Carole Littlejohn, who worked as a cleaner at St Budock School near Falmouth in the 1980s, told me, 'I heard these footsteps when working there in the evening… above our heads, and they were very heavy like hobnailed boots. The odd thing is this part of the school property had a pitched roof so nobody could walk on it. In the old days there had been a verandah, and those ghostly footsteps must have belonged to that time.'

In two of our haunted properties in Cornwall, the Bush Inn at Morwenstow and the Tredethy Country House Hotel at Helland Bridge on the edge of Bodmin Moor, ghosts have climbed the respective staircases at their original levels, ignoring structural changes made at later dates.

Peter Underwood, the Life President of The Ghost Club

Society, posed the question 'Why are so many stairways haunted?' in his book *Peter Underwood's Guide to Ghosts and Haunted Places*. He answered his own question with the following suggestion: 'Can it be they form a sort of vortex or whirlpool that sometimes gathers up psychic energy and becomes the centre of such activity in the house? Certainly it is a fact that the most haunted part of a house is likely to be the stairway area and there are far more haunted stairways than any other individual part of the house.'

Back in the 1960s in North Cornwall I came to know a remarkable Tintagel character, Charlie Bennett, who removed warts from people and ringworm from cattle with such success that the local doctor and veterinary surgeon recommended him – which was quite something at that time. Charlie told me that one day he was walking through St Nectan's Glen, probably the most haunted valley in the whole of the West Country, when he 'stopped for a breather and sat on a fallen tree… suddenly weird mocking laughter broke out… it were as if an invisible somebody was saying "Charlie Bennett, you need a rest – not as young as you were!"'

On another occasion Charlie was walking up the glen – this time in early evening when odd things tend to happen hereabouts – and he was suddenly aware of sobbing. He searched all over the place but he could find nobody. Then there was another sound: the same mocking laughter he had encountered on the earlier visit. 'I continued to search until the light began to go,' he recalled, 'but no success.' He could not find the source of either the mocking laughter or the sobbing. 'A weird place' was Charlie's summing up.

Someone else who had bizarre experiences in St Nectan's was the potter Pip Everard. She and a friend heard 'strange chanting by invisible monks in the glen'. Pip also told me how she had heard beautiful music coming from an empty church nearby, St Piran's.

From monks to billiards… Ken Snowdon and I were doing a radio series entitled 'Ghost hunt' and one of our interviews took place at the haunted Bush Inn at Morwenstow. During the interview in a small upstairs room we picked up some strange, inexplicable sounds. When we played back the interview they were still there – like the clicking of billiard or snooker balls during a game. They were so real that anyone standing outside the door would have assumed somebody was playing a sporadic game. The Bush cat was with us in the room and he 'followed' these strange sounds as they travelled along one wall. All four of us present had no doubts about the genuine yet puzzling nature of the clicking.

As music has a significant role in most religions, it is no surprise that there are cases of ghostly organ playing in churches and chapels – not that such ghostly sounds are limited to religious buildings. Not long ago I had a report of a phantom violinist in a private house in North Cornwall. More than one person has told me of uncanny music emanating from inside St Michael's Church, Brentor, when it was empty. Nationally there are claims from people like Rosemary Brown for the source of their musical inspirations coming from long dead musicians such as Chopin and Schubert, Beethoven and Debussy.

Totally unexpected sightings of ghosts are particularly exciting for the investigator if more than one person has the same experience at the same time. A high percentage of shared sightings come about in a very matter of fact way: nothing planned and certainly not part of any recognised ghost hunt in any sense. Here is an extract from a letter I received in February 1994. It was written by Alison Hamlin of Northwich, Cheshire, who had just returned from a weekend break in the Land's End area of West Cornwall:

'While travelling back from St Ives at about 7 pm on Sunday night we came back through St Just and past the Land's End Aerodrome. Shortly after the Aerodrome we came round a sharp right-hand bend and I saw out of the corner of my eye somebody on the road. I slowed down quite a bit as our van takes up most of the road; when I looked properly there was nobody there. Within seconds of this a silvery-white shape moved quickly across the road from left to right, then moved up into the air for 10 to 15 feet, then dropped down on the other side of the hedge. The shape was only about 2 feet across and didn't have a definite edge to it. I said to my boyfriend who was in the passenger seat, "What was that?" He said jokingly: "I think we've just seen a ghost". We had a bit of a laugh about it, thinking we were seeing things. When we got back to the campsite we asked our friend who was travelling in a van behind us if he saw anything. Without telling him what we saw, he described exactly the same thing, although he didn't see the person in the road that I saw.

'By this time we were getting a bit worried about what we had seen and it didn't seem to be funny any more.

'Later on we went into the Wreckers Inn (Terry and Myra are friends of ours). We told Holly (their daughter) about our encounter and she said "It's nothing new. I know quite a few people who have seen it recently."'

I have long believed that dates – anniversaries – are sometimes significant in manifestations. A report in *Psychic News*, published in September 1966, confirmed the belief: 'The highlight of the séance was the purported presence and communications from Lord Hugh Dowding, Chief of Fighter Command during the Battle of Britain. It is significant that he came through on the very day (Sept 15th) that Commemoration Services for the Battle of Britain were being held across the country.

'Lord Dowding was of course a dedicated Spiritualist whilst on earth. As soon as he arrived it became apparent that he has a great sense of humour – which rather surprised most of us. But as well as joking and playing about he also brought great words of wisdom.

'One lady present who had known Dowding well during the war confirmed his identity… The materialised form had shaken hands with her and recalled the time spent together during the war. On leaving her he kissed her hand. She also confirmed his great sense of humour which surprised us as his public persona was rather stiff and severe.

'Lord Dowding also shook many other hands and even wandered behind the back row patting many on the shoulder as he passed by.'

Ongoing stories of strange happenings

Jamaica Inn at Bolventor, high on Bodmin Moor, is the classic case of an ongoing story of the paranormal.

I have known Jamaica for more than forty years and over all those years its supernatural reputation has rumbled on. There have perhaps been times when these bizarre happenings have gone quiet – but only for a while. The years 1995 and 1996 produced a string of manifestations in and around the inn.

A former manager, Tony Turner, told me how on several nights he heard discussions going on – very audible discussions, but in a language he could not understand. Furthermore these conversations were heard on occasions when only Tony and his wife were in residence. He also explained how the sound of horses coming into the courtyard at night had been heard by various people but, on investigation, no animals were there. Zoe Hodges, a later manager at Jamaica, told me of a visitor who complained about the noise made by a baby in the next door bedroom. She said the baby had cried a great deal during the night – but Zoe assured me there was no baby or small child staying on the night in question.

Val Wadge, who cooks and has been working at the inn for more than twenty-five years, told me she had seen a strange figure in the du Maurier restaurant. 'There were four of us sitting at a table by the door... we'd done a function and I was sitting with Mr and Mrs Turner and another member of the staff, having something to eat. Suddenly I saw a figure in green and black come through the door and go out again. I saw him again outside through the window. None of the others saw him and Mrs Turner explained that this particular door was locked, but I saw him all right. A man I should say, and wearing this green and black cloak. My daughter has also seen him standing by the fridge. He seems to keep to this area – in the old days it was the stabling – and I've felt his presence on other occasions. I'd be working in the kitchen and somehow *know* he was in the restaurant. I've come through to look; nobody here but some smoke in the air and I knew no staff or guest have been here smoking.

'There have been other noises… bumps and cups rattling, and it's not just me. One member of staff saw a man standing by the big fire in the main bar and another looked one day across at the cottage on the other side of the road… our annex… a woman and two children were looking out of an upstairs window. He went across and opened up the cottage, but nobody was there.'

Collectively these strange happenings add up to something substantial, and the fact that they have been seen and heard on different dates by different people reinforces Jamaica's haunted reputation. There is something or some things – or some person or persons – that refuse to go away. Some unfinished business perhaps? As for the hoofbeats in the yard outside, could they be psychic echoes of the past when coaches used to call here? Or did Daphne du Maurier base her famous novel on fact? If Jamaica had been the base of a smuggling operation, then we do know horses and ponies would have been involved moving the smuggled goods swiftly inland at night. Truth is, the old inn poses some intriguing questions – and possibilities.

I have done two television interviews here – one in the Daphne du Maurier Room – and on both occasions I spoke about the atmosphere of Jamaica Inn. Out of season, or any time when it is very quiet, you get a feeling you are on the edge of the unknown. There seems to be a presence here and you feel it only requires one more thing to happen before it comes out and shows the reality of the phenomena. I have felt this presence on the staircase, in the corridor upstairs and out in the courtyard. At night when there are no people about, this courtyard undergoes a personality change. You may see nothing unusual but there is an impression, an influence which is not quite of this world.

Ghost hunting is a matter of being in the right place at the right time. At Jamaica Inn I have had that good luck. On two

Ghost Club Society studies I saw the same man twice on each visit: a powerful dark character, like a rugby forward, hurrying away in the Stable Bar. He moved at such a pace you felt he was responding to a command or the arrival of a coach. On all four occasions he dashed in the direction of the courtyard and our mediums later confirmed he worked with horses in the old coaching days. Significantly too, all four sightings were observed by another member of our group – so no question of an over-heated imagination or a trick of shadow.

All of which reinforces my belief that teamwork is essential, but preferably a small team – six to eight people is perfect.

During a quiet session at Jamaica, Paul Richards, a fellow Cornish member, and I picked up snippets of a strange conversation some distance away, spoken in a foreign language, probably French, soft and confidential in manner. Lisa Turpin, a member of the inn staff who was with us, thought this overheard conversation did not relate to any guests or other staff – as it was just after 3 am.

The diversity of the paranormal happenings at Jamaica remind us there are different kinds of ghost and no single clearcut explanation fits them all. Jamaica teaches us another lesson too: there are forces about which we know next to nothing *and* forces over which we have no control. It is not only a fascinating place for the ghost hunter, but somewhere where a major investigative breakthrough will almost certainly occur.

Penhallow Manor is another such place. In August 1996 I was involved in doing research for a television programme, an instalment of 'The Ghost Hunters' series for Sky. One of the locations featured was Penhallow Manor at Altarnun on the edge of Bodmin Moor. Like Jamaica Inn, Penhallow is an ongoing story.

For the programme I suggested Shirley Wallis be invited to take part. I have a high regard for Shirley's psychic detective work. She is an exponent of psycho-expansion and therefore has this extraordinary ability to travel back in time. Moreover she is a lady of absolute integrity. It was, in fact, Shirley's first ever visit to the village which Dame Daphne du Maurier immortalised in her riveting Cornish novel *Jamaica Inn*, and her revelations during the recording of the programme astounded all of us. She not only picked up the presence of the former vicar, but revealed a triangular love affair between the parson, his wife and young mistress. She gave detailed descriptions of life at the rectory in those earlier times – the music and the books, and how the people looked and related to one another.

She also picked up a nearby death and the cause of that death. It was a *tour de force* in travelling back in time.

The then proprietress Julia Cubbage and previous owners all made contributions to the televised episode, recalling incidents which collectively mean a good deal of paranormal activity has taken place – and continues to go on in and around the building. But I hasten to reassure prospective guests that Penhallow retains a beautiful atmosphere. I first knew this Georgian style house more than thirty years ago when it was a rectory and the same serenity reigns.

Pehallow Manor and Jamaica Inn, in their different ways, demonstrate an important paranormal fact. Some buildings may change their function – even change their name as in the case of Penhallow – but they retain something of the past and that something is so strong that some people pick up ghostly happenings in the here and now.

Some Bristol hauntings

I spent the greater part of my National Service at Horfield Barracks, some thirteen years before my conversion to the paranormal – and yet even in those early days I felt that Bristol, in particular the older parts, had such a strong sense of the past that it was as though I was caught up in some kind of time warp.

I remember seeing my first county cricket on the county ground at Bristol and I felt an extra dimension to it all, thinking of and seeing in the eye of my imagination great cricketers like Dr W G Grace and Gilbert Jessop performing historic deeds with bat and ball on the field.

And when I went to the theatre I found myself relating to distinguished actors of the past.

The Theatre Royal, Bristol, is reputed to be the oldest theatre in the land: it has been in almost continuous use since it opened its doors in 1766. Consequently, later on when my interest in the supernatural was deepening, I was not surprised to learn it is haunted and one of its ghosts is that of Sarah Siddons, who acted here between 1778 and 1782.

During subsequent investigations into the paranormal, and especially the ghostly field, I have come to this conclusion: some areas strong in atmosphere appear to trigger psychic phenomena. Bristol is a good example. There have been happenings in and around the city which defy all rational explanation.

Through research and reading over the years I have come to know a good deal about the historical ghosts of Bristol but, for the purpose of this project, I decided to try to find out about more modern hauntings in the city. The *Bristol Evening Post* kindly published my appeal for any firsthand experiences. It brought forth some interesting cases.

The first was a very prompt response from Rachel Mann, an Aquarian writing from Bishopston. I later spoke on the telephone with Rachel. Her encounters with the supernatural took place at Maxwell's Restaurant (now a bank), The Mall, Bristol, where Rachel was a chef-manager: 'Whilst I have never actually seen a ghost, your letter in the *Evening Post* reminded me of what could be described as paranormal activity at the restaurant I worked at between June 1989 and October 1990. There were many strange things which happened, not only to myself and not only in that period of time.

'When I began working at the restaurant I was informed there was a resident ghost which people had felt touch them and which regularly spilt salt on the tables during the night. I was also informed that a medium had detected a fire in the building in the past which may have killed someone.

'My own experiences were as follows: I decided, being a sceptic, to test the salt story. One evening I made sure I wiped all the tables myself before locking up. I told no one I was doing the experiment but surely enough the next morning when I was the first person in the building there was salt spilt on several of the tables.

'The second experience involves another occasion when I was alone in the building. I was in the kitchen of the restaurant where I could not see the front door. I did not hear the entrance bell of the front door go but I heard a chair scrape back in the restaurant area. I dashed out thinking a customer had come into the restaurant early, but there was no one there. There was however a chair pushed away from one of the tables. I knew this was odd because I had personally pushed all chairs under the tables at the beginning of my shift. I am no longer a sceptic...'

Catherine Davies told me about a strange experience around 1973-74 '... when I worked as a theatre orderly at the radiotherapy centre near Bristol Royal Infirmary. My job was to make sure that all the equipment, lamps, etc were clean and ready before operations. Attached to the theatre of course were hand basins for the surgeons and it was between these two areas that I saw the ghost – a plain cotton shroud that walked along as if on wheels, gliding along, no face but the form of a human being. Mine was a side view. I went quickly into the next room where my colleague looked after the x-ray department. I told her what I had seen and she mentioned she had heard a rustling sound, looked around... but nobody was there. That picture of the ghost has stayed with me ever since.'

Angela Pollard, who lives in the St George area of the city, recalled three quite separate and seemingly unrelated sightings – the third in December 1996. 'The first sighting was when I was 14 and it happened in my parents' house: a little girl dressed in a white pinafore and wearing old fashioned boots. My second sighting was in 1996 when I was sharing a house and saw a cavalier soldier walk through the wall. My third sighting was later that same year. I was about to go to sleep when our dog Grace started to bark and growl. I looked over to the corner of the room and saw what looked like a monk... he stayed there for quite a while.'

Finally, there was a shared sighting from Brian Taylor of Thornbury.

'On October 18th 1995 at approximately 11.30 pm I was driving along Kington Lane in the older part of Thornbury.

'Suddenly I was forced to brake as something that can only be described as a 5 foot grey mist of non-human form, but of some definite shape, was in the road. "It" was startled by our approach and quickly went across the road and disappeared into a 6 foot stone wall. It seemed to hesitate as if pushing its way through… which allowed us to clearly see it entering the wall that had no holes or gaps in it. It was definitely not an animal and did not jump over or burrow under the wall. We actually saw it go *through* the *solid* wall.

'We looked into the field that it had entered and saw a herd of very disturbed cows bellowing noisily and chasing after something… but there was nothing there for them to chase. As a countryman I know this was unusual behaviour for cattle at night.'

Some reflections

Ghost hunting can produce strange twists and turns.

Some four years ago Lynne Barks invited me to her house just off the Camelford-Wadebridge road to hear about some unusual canine goings-on. The house, set in lovely green countryside, has a peaceful atmosphere.

Lynne told me: 'My husband and I were sitting here in the lounge recently when we heard a dog scratching at the door and then heard it running up the stairs.

'We went to investigate but there was no dog upstairs and our own dog Lucy was fast asleep in another downstairs room.'

Lynne reckoned they have heard these dog movements – usually the noise of two dogs – more than twenty times in the last four years.

'Visitors have heard them too and there are never any paw marks. By the noise they make, they must be two large dogs –

but we never see any animal.

'My husband can be quite a cynic on the subject of the super-natural, but even he has to admit there is something very strange about these noises. There simply isn't a logical explanation.

'The odd thing is our dog and another who died recently have never reacted to these other animal sounds. It seems only human beings hear them and only when sitting in our lounge.'

It was all very interesting, but the oddest fact is that after my visit the phantom dogs were never heard again. I am no exorcist but it seems as if our conversation somehow exorcised the hauntings.

Was my visit and no more dog sounds coincidence? Or did Lynne's telling somehow release the dogs? Have they gone on – many of us believe animals go beyond the thing we call death – or had they, like numerous other ghosts, played out their time? This does happen: there are many instances where a ghost has faded and finally disappeared from the scene.

Anyway, those two dogs remain a North Cornwall mystery.

In October 2002 there was an exceptional development in the paranormal saga at Tredethy House. I had arranged for a party of Ghost Club Society members to pay a visit and our medium, Pamela Smith-Rawnsley, down at the foot of the haunted staircase, made contact with the spirit of a man. One would have assumed it might have been the butler who has been seen in that vicinity or Prince Chula himself, a one-time owner of the property.

It turned out to be neither, but an English gentleman called Thomas Smith who had supplied curtains and furnishings to the Royal Palace of Rama V in Siam in the second half of the 1800s.

To our surprise and delight, he was identified as Trevor Kenward's great grandfather – and only Trevor knew of the family link. It was an extraordinary feat of mediumship and the curious thing is: Trevor Kenward, one of the most experienced ghost hunters in Britain today, had come to Cornwall with no thought of linking up with his relative.

I still vividly recall my first all-night investigation under the leadership of Peter Underwood, our Ghost Club Society Life President. It was September 1988 at Curry Mallet Manor House in Somerset, and proved to be a remarkable baptism. Objects were moved, strange sounds heard and my first seance observed – a fascinating cocktail of experience.

Peter kindly asked me for a report of the night. Here is part of that report:

'Though no ghosts were seen, a number of interesting things did happen, nothing dramatic, but collectively they add up to *something*.

'I am very responsive to atmosphere and found the Manor House strong in atmosphere. In certain parts there was a strong sense of the past – this was especially so in the garden. Outside, during the night, one felt right on the frontier of the unknown. You had the feeling that something of a supernatural nature could happen at any moment – and this was not mere wishful thinking.

'I am sure spirits from the past do come to that garden. There may be some unfinished business or they may have loved the place – or someone there – very deeply. And who can blame them coming back to that lovely corner of Somerset?'

Quite my most spectacular sighting was at Pengersick Castle, on the rim of Mount's Bay, during another Ghost Club Society study.

This phantom lady with an aristocratic air came out of the wall of the haunted bedroom: she was tallish, wearing a grey or light coloured dress that went down to the floor. She was slim, a fact revealed by her ornate belt, and she was giving the impression that she was looking for someone or something. One particular oddity is that a tiny torch seemed to be glowing from the region of her navel. The fact that seven people out of ten present saw her is impressive.

I have often thought about the three people who did not see her. Were they perhaps too tense, too keyed up? Ghost hunting, like batting at cricket, requires relaxed concentration.

Getting back to dogs – a man living in a cottage in Devon had a dog which reacted strangely in the evenings. The dog would suddenly sit bolt upright, stare at the door and then, in gaze, he would follow an invisible something across the room.

When the dog died, his owner bought a successor, the same breed but from another part of the country. Almost immediately the second dog began behaving in precisely the same way – and only in the evenings.

It was such an uncanny replay that I and Pamela Smith-Rawnsley, with two other members of the Ghost Club Society, were invited to the cottage one evening in September 2002 – and Pamela quickly established connection with the spirit of a monk who formerly lived there. Moreover the dog in residence seemed very in tune with Pamela's mediumship; so much so he led her to a spot in the cottage where the monk had regularly said his prayers and meditated.

As the future unfolds, we ghost hunters are looking for major breakthroughs – such as ghosts on film and sounds on tape, evidence that will satisfy the most cynical scientist.

I hope to be around when that moment comes.